LET'S MAKE A DIFFERENCE:

WE CAN HELP
ORANGUTANS

SAVE COINS FOR CAUSES WE CAN HELP!

BBM BOOKS

, Newport Beach, CA

KIDS WITH COINS

Layout, cover and illustrations by Phil Velikan www.findphil.com
Editorial assistance provided by Dorothy Chambers
Packaged by Wish Publishing

Printed in China
10 9 8 7 6 5 4 3 2 1

Published by BBM Books

Photography credits for Shutterstock.com

Page 1 ©aodaodaodaod/Shutterstock.com
Page 3 ©szefei/Shutterstock.com
Page 4 ©Eric Esselee/Shutterstock.com
Page 5 ©Eric Gevaert/Shutterstock.com
Page 6 ©Eric Gevaert/Shutterstock.com
Page 7 ©ilolob/Shutterstock.com
Page 8 © Y.F. Wong/Shutterstock.com
Page 9 Ivy ©Lim Yong Hian/Shutterstock.com
    Bananas ©Tatiana Popova/Shutterstock.com
    Bark ©Vitaly Titov & Maria Sidelnikova/
        Shutterstock.com
    Durian ©WuttgataP/Shutterstock.com
    Bugs ©Pan Xunbin/Shutterstock.com
    Jackfruit ©ahnhuynh/Shutterstock.com

Page 10 ©Peter Wollinga/Shutterstock.com
Page 11 ©Matthew Cole/Shutterstock.com
Page 12 ©Wong Hock Weng/Shutterstock.com
Page 13 Umbrella leaf ©Alvin Tjiprahardja/
        orangutanrepublik.org
Page 14 ©Tatiana Morozova/Shutterstock.com
Page 15 Trees ©aodaodaodaod/Shutterstock.com
        Sign ©riekephotos/Shutterstock.com
Page 16 ©Yuri Arcurs/Shutterstock.com
Page 17 ©tristan tan/Shutterstock.com
Page 18 ©A.S. Zain/Shutterstock.com
Page 19 ©A. S. Zain/Shutterstock.com
Page 20 ©holstphoto/Shutterstock.com
Page 21 ©archidea/Shutterstock.com

Page 22 ©Nagy-Bagoly Arpad/Shutterstock.com
Page 23 ©Helder Almeida/Shutterstock.com
Page 24 Bank ©Rade Kovac/Shutterstock.com
        Teller ©Sanjay Deva/Shutterstock.com
Page 25 ©Janelle Lugge/Shutterstock.com
Page 26 ©Uryadnikov Sergey/Shutterstock.com
Page 27 ©Nathape/Shutterstock.com
Page 28 ©Peter Zijlstra/Shutterstock.com
Page 29 ©Pu Su Lan/Shutterstock.com
Page 30 ©Uryadnikov Sergey/Shutterstock.com
Page 31 ©LindyCro/Shutterstock.com

Special thanks to Wish Publishing for their help bringing this book into being.

For
**Dr. Nancy Briggs for her
love of and dedication
to orangutans**

This is Malcolm.

Malcolm is an orangutan. Orangutans are a lot like you: smart, funny, handy. They live with their mother, just like you do. They even like to ride piggy back!

3

4

Once there were hundreds of thousands of orangutans living all over Southeast Asia and China. Now there are only a few thousand living on just two islands: Borneo and Sumatra. The orangutans are endangered. "Endangered" means that if people don't help them, the orangutans will someday disappear.

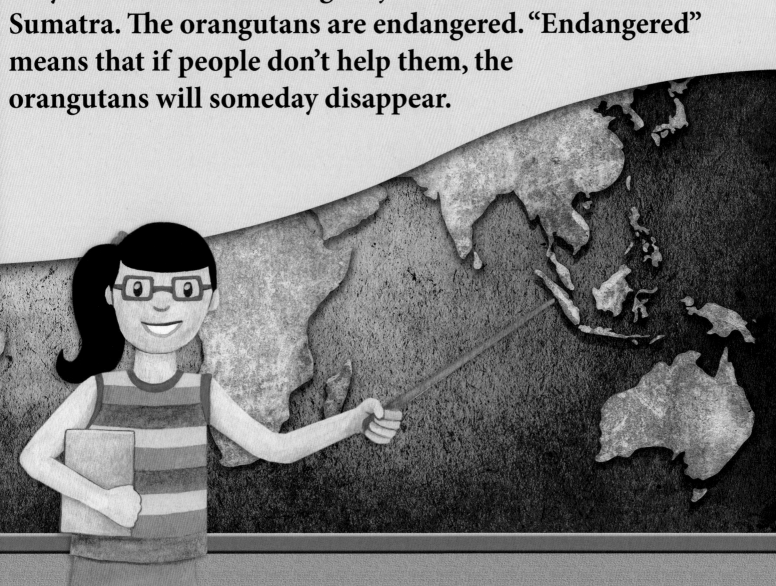

Why are they **endangered?**

Orangutans live in the canopy — the top branchy layer — of trees, which along with the entire tropical rainforest ecosysytem, is quickly disappearing.

Orangutans eat the plants that grow in the rainforest.

Things orangutans eat:

- durian fruit
- jack fruit
- leaves
- bark
- vines
- flowers
- bugs

Did you know that orangutans are smart enough to make a glove out of leaves so they can touch plants with thorns? Orangutans are also polite – they use leaves like napkins to wipe their sticky chins.

Orangutan Fun Fact

Not just birds have nests. Orangutans will build a nest every night high in the trees, to sleep in. Sometimes they even add a roof of leaves!

Not only do the orangutans need the rainforest to eat, they need it for shelter, too. They sleep in nests built high in the tree branches.

The canopy is also their playground. They can travel all over the rainforest just by swinging from branch to branch.

Why is the canopy **disappearing?**

Many years ago, people started coming into the rainforest and cutting down trees to make paper, to build palm oil plantations, and to make homes for themselves. They didn't realize that when they cut down the trees they were destroying the homes of the orangutans.

Eviction Notice TODAY

Orangutan Fun Fact

Who needs an umbrella? When it rains or the sun is too hot, orangutans will find and use a leafy branch to provide portable shade or shelter.

11

Today there are laws protecting the rainforests, but so much damage has already been done that the orangutans are in trouble. Luckily there are people who have made it their job to protect the orangutans.

PLEASE TAKE NOTHING BUT PICTURES LEAVE NOTHING BUT FOOTPRINTS

Who works to **help them?**

All over the world, there are groups of people who work to protect the orangutans and their rainforest homes in Borneo and Sumatra. They study orangutans to understand what they need to live, and then they teach people how to protect orangutans and other animals in danger.

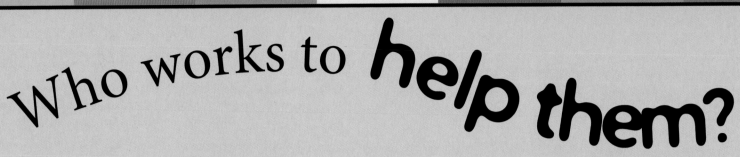

Orangutan Fun Fact

Orangutans have opposable thumbs, which means they can touch each of their fingers with their thumb.

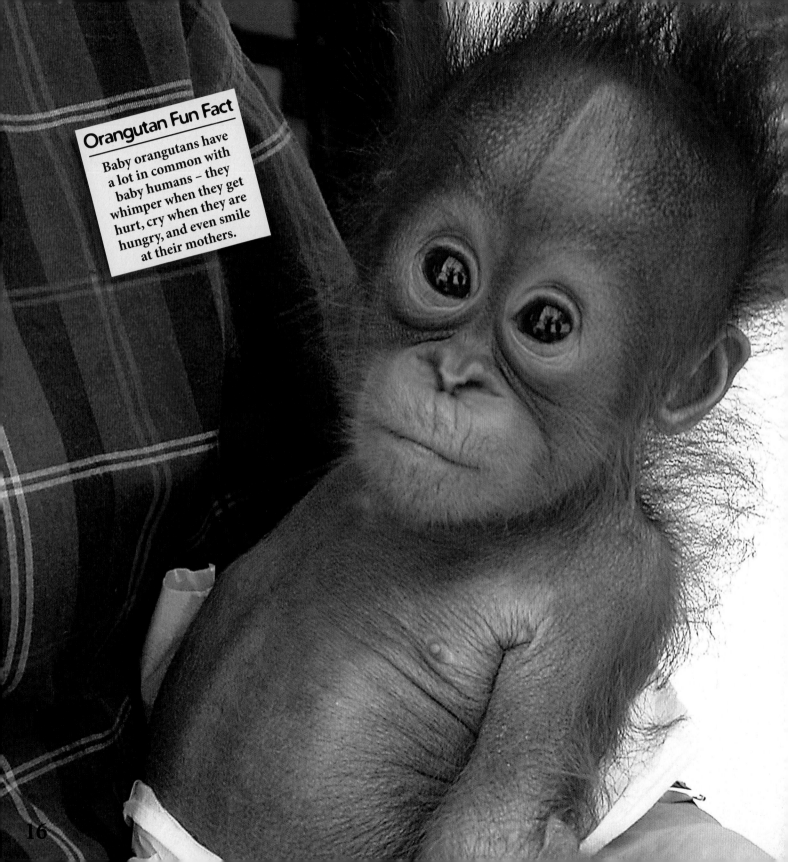

Orangutan Fun Fact

Baby orangutans have a lot in common with baby humans – they whimper when they get hurt, cry when they are hungry, and even smile at their mothers.

16

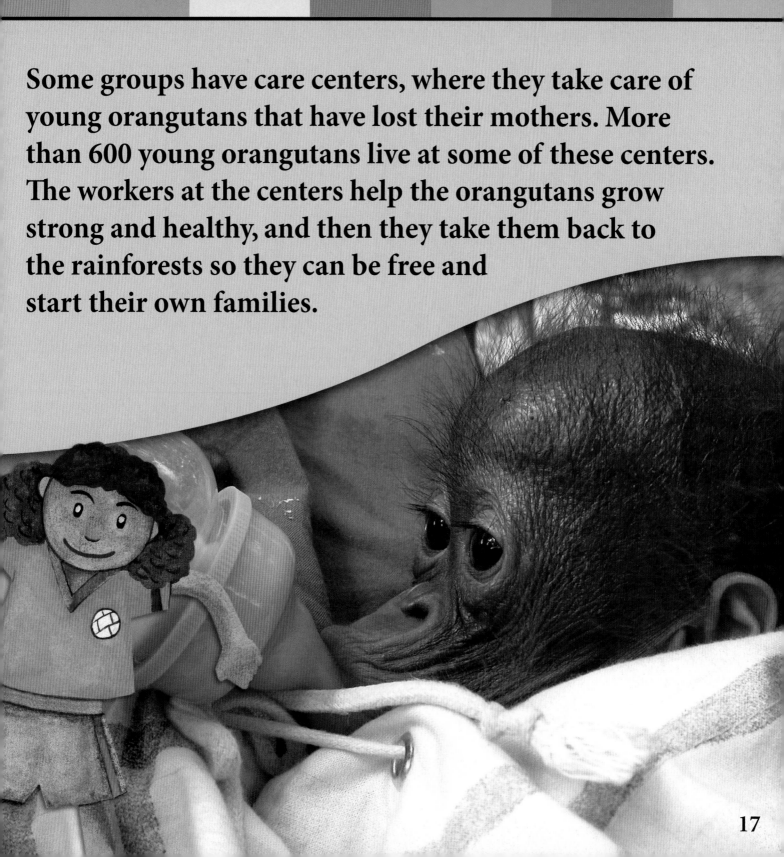

Some groups have care centers, where they take care of young orangutans that have lost their mothers. More than 600 young orangutans live at some of these centers. The workers at the centers help the orangutans grow strong and healthy, and then they take them back to the rainforests so they can be free and start their own families.

How can you **help them?**

What can you do to help? Lots! These organizations need people all over the world to help care for the orangutans. If you live near or travel to Indonesia, you can even visit a care center.

Even if you can't visit, you can help. You know how you are always finding coins on the sidewalk, or between the couch cushions, or under your bed? If you start saving all of those coins, you can save up enough money to help take care of the orangutans! An easy way to do it would be to get an empty jug or jar and drop all the coins you find into it. You can even ask your friends and family to add to the jug every time they have extra coins in their pocket.

After you have filled the jug, take your coins to a bank and have the teller exchange your coins for dollars. Give these dollars to an adult you trust and ask him or her to use a credit card to make a donation for that amount to one of the organizations listed on the back page of this book.

Orangutan Fun Fact

An orangutan mom spends at least seven years providing constant care and attention to her baby. She will only have another baby after the first one is fully grown and can live on its own.

Orangutan Fun Fact

Orangutans really are great swingers! They swing arm over arm through the forest better than any other kind of ape.

What will your money do?

Some of your money will go to help feed the orangutans, some will help fund research on how to protect them better from diseases and other natural problems, and some will help fund educational programs to teach people how to live in and around the orangutans without hurting their environment.

Another thing you can do to help the orangutans is very simple: Tell your parents that you only want to use products that have sustainable palm oil. Palm oil is in lots of delicious foods like ice cream, cookies, candy and popcorn. It is often grown on land that used to be rainforest. However, palm oil production does not have to cause harm to orangutans and other wildlife. If a food you really love is made with palm oil, write to the company that makes it and tell them you would love for them to use only sustainable palm oil and help you protect the orangutans.

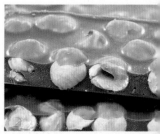

USE ONLY SUSTAINABLE PALM OIL

Orangutan Fun Fact

If you see an orangutan puckering up his lips and making a smacking noise, it doesn't mean he wants a kiss! That means he would like someone to leave him alone.

Remember that you can help – no matter how short or tall or young or old, we all have the ability to help one another. Even if you start small with that penny you found on the sidewalk yesterday, you'll be surprised how quickly you can save up enough money to help an orangutan like Malcolm.

Here are some organizations that work to protect the orangutans and their home, the rainforest.

World Wildlife Fund
www.wwf.org
WWF's mission is to stop the degradation of the planet's natural environment and to build a future in which humans live in harmony with nature by conserving the world's biological diversity, ensuring that the use of renewable natural resources is sustainable and promoting the reduction of pollution and wasteful consumption.

Orangutan Foundation International
www.orangutan.org
The mission of the Orangutan Foundation International is to support the conservation, protection and understanding of orangutans and their rainforest habitat while caring for ex-captive orangutan orphans as they make their way back to the forest.

Orangutan Outreach
www.redapes.org
Orangutan Outreach's mission is to protect orangutans in their native habitat while providing care for orphaned and displaced orangutans until they can be returned to their natural environment.

ARKive.org
www.ARKive.org
The ARKive website is a collection of the best photos, video clips and fact-files of endangered animals from around the world.

Orang Utan Republik Foundation
www.orangutanrepublik.org
The Orang Utan Republik Foundation works to save the orangutans of Indonesia through conservation education, outreach initiatives and innovative collaborative programs that inspire and call people to action.

The Nature Conservancy
www.nature.org
The Nature Conservancy is working with you to make a positive impact around the world in more than 30 countries, all 50 United States and your backyard.

Orang-Utans in Not e.V. (Orangutans in Peril)
www.orang-utans-in-not.org/engl/
Orang-Utans in Not e.V. (Orangutans in Peril) was founded in Leipzig, Germany in 2007 and aims to protect the last of the wild orangutans on the Southeast Asian islands of Borneo and Sumatra.

Save the Orangutan
www.savetheorangutan.org
This organization works to raise funds, work in partnerships and provide public education and awareness to save the orangutan.

The Great Ape Heart Project
www.greatapeheartproject.org
The mission of the Great Ape Heart Project (GAHP) is to investigate and understand heart disease in great apes. Heart disease is one of the top health concerns for orangutans and other apes that live in zoos.

International Union for the Conservation of Nature Red List of Threatened Species™
www.iucnredlist.org
The IUCN works to provide information and analyses on the status, trends and threats to species in order to inform and catalyse action for biodiversity conservation.

The views expressed in this publication do not necessarily reflect those of IUCN or other participating organizations.

To See Orangutans in the United States, You Can Visit:

The Indianapolis Zoo
www.indianapoliszoo.com
Visitors to the Indianapolis Zoo's International Orangutan Center™ engage with orangutans through a dynamic exhibit space; are enlightened about opportunities for human/orangutan interaction and learning; and are empowered by providing information on how they can directly affect orangutan conservation in the wild.

The San Diego Zoo
www.sandiegozoo.org
The 100-acre San Diego Zoo is a not-for-profit conservation organization accredited by the Association of Zoos and Aquariums and the American Association of Museums. The Zoo is well known for its lush, naturalistic habitats and unique animal encounters.